10 little theories
about Argentines

MARTINA KIST

In collaboration with Hanneke Vaanhold
Illustrations by Juan Manuel Gordillo

Original title:
10 pequeñas teorías sobre los Argentinos. Una mirada extranjera.

First published in Argentina by Editorial del Nuevo Extremo, 2016

ISBN: 978-987-609-658-4

Published in English by Pollok Glen Publishing, 2020

ISBN: 978-1-9164486-3-6

Translated from Spanish by the author and her daughter Nina

Cover: uses image from @ mauromod (Depositphotos)

POLLOK GLEN
PUBLISHING

To whom this book is directed

This book is for Argentines who interact with foreigners, particularly at work. For foreigners who move to Argentina and want to understand their new environment better. And for anyone who, in one way or another, is interested in differences between cultures and in the impression made by Argentines.

I am not crazy

"Don't you read the papers in Brazil? Don't you see that the situation in Argentina is bad? Why is it then that you decided to come here?" That, a Brazilian friend tells me, is how she was welcomed by the other moms at her daughter's school. "You always have to defend yourself and explain why you are here" says an Italian.

As for myself, I settled in Buenos Aires a little over a year ago. Before that, I lived in seven different countries and had never experienced being systematically called crazy by the inhabitants for wanting to move to their land (or, as Argentines prefer to call it, to "este país"[1])

In their view, it seems that only two reasons can justify your wanting to live here: either you are in love, or you have a mental problem.

Although I will confess to being in love with my Argentine husband, working on this book proved to be very useful to gauge my mental health. Because I don't just live here, to make matters worse... I also love the country and its people! Since I spent the past 25 years of my life carrying out opinion research and am a big fan of cultural topics, the idea of this book emerged almost naturally: using standard questions, I would interview

---

[1] "this country" – pronounced with a disdainful tone.

approximately 50 foreigners who live in Argentina to gather their impressions.

Fortunately, when I compared my experience to that of others, I realized I am not that crazy, or at least I am not the only one. Along the way, I reached a better understanding of what characterizes "this place" and summoned up the courage to write **my little theories about Argentines**.

I am sharing them with all those who, after a possible first reaction of defense, will not be afraid to find themselves in these pages. This is the Argentine I see and like so much.

PS: As Ted Stanger said in *Sacrés français* (an essay about the French and for the French): "My vision may surprise you and that's normal: one can look in the mirror a thousand times without ever seeing oneself".

Rumor has it Chesterton was once asked
what he thought about the French,
to which he replied:
"I don't know. I don't know them all".

Preliminary warning

The people interviewed in this book, and all those who took part in it, know perfectly well that it is impossible to make generalizations about a culture and that every member of this culture is different. All Argentines are not as we describe them and probably none of them completely fits the profile that is provided here.

If you feel that my view on Argentines is too general, caricatured and coarse, that my outside perspective overlooks particularities, then you are correct. My main objective is not to reveal the truth about Argentine identity (me, a Dutch national, of all people!) but to amuse and (perhaps) make you think.

Likewise, the foreigners interviewed in the process of making this book do not represent the opinion of all their fellow countrymen and women: an Italian is not representative of all Italians, and so on. But all of them live or have lived in Argentina, be it for a short period or as their permanent home.

Lastly, I want to clarify that when we refer to Argentine customs, neither the foreigners interviewed nor I are necessarily suggesting that things are better in our own countries!

Main characters

THE ARGENTINES. Or, more precisely, the people of the city of Buenos Aires (*porteños*) and its province (*bonaerenses*). Most foreigners interviewed live in or around the capital, so that's where their impressions were formed.

56 FOREIGNERS who accepted to shed light on my research by sharing their experiences in Argentina and with Argentines. They were contacted through recommendations of people to whom I spoke about my project, or specifically sought out in international schools, specialized restaurants, community neighborhoods, etc.

ME. Martina Kist (my birth name is Anne Martijntje but it is unpronounceable outside of The Netherlands), 51 years old, mother of four, economist. I was born in the Netherlands to Dutch parents. My journey across the world started when I was only three years old. I lived in Poland, the United States, Switzerland, the Netherlands, Mexico, France (where I studied and spent many years), again in the United States and now Argentina. I speak five languages but dream without words. I believe I was unable to take root in any of these places because of the pleasure I found in this cosmopolitan life, which also developed my strong interest for cultural differences. I learned lots of things along the way, but there is only one thing I know for sure: everybody thinks differently, but at the same time, everybody thinks that they are right!

My work method

Selecting the people interviewed

My 56 interviewees come from various countries. Some will only stay, or have stayed, in Argentina for a short time, others came here to settle down permanently.

In order to reflect all the phases of acculturation[2], I chose people who had been in Argentina for less than a year, some who had been here between 1 and 2 years, and some who had arrived more than 3 years ago. The idea behind this was to collect both the first impressions, and the subsequent ones.

The majority of foreigners interviewed had also lived in other countries (apart from their birth country) before coming to Argentina, which gives the results more contrast, since people who have spent time in different

---

[2] It is said that during the first months of living abroad, reactions are essentially of awe and exaltation and that foreigners show a spontaneous openness towards the new culture. After the first year, the person starts to show resistance to the new culture but is also transformed by it: this is the questioning phase. After 2 or 3 years (depending on the person, sometimes this phase never occurs), a certain integration/acculturation begins, due to the better understanding of the environment.

societies usually transcend cultural barriers and identify significant differences more easily.

Participating countries

The countries of origin were chosen according to my interests and experience. This study does not claim to be based on a representative sample, but rather on a large array of viewpoints in which I included:

- Countries whose culture I know well enough (like the Netherlands, France and the United States) but which also somehow influenced Argentine history. The Argentine constitution of 1853, for instance, was inspired by the French constitution as well as the American (cf. Saenz Quesada, p. 339.). The Netherlands were the first country to recognize Argentina's independence after 1816. And then there is Maxima of course, currently the Queen of the Netherlands and from Argentina!

- Countries which represent the largest migratory influx to Argentina, like Italy and Spain.

- Countries which culture I don't know that well but which are major players in today's world, like China and Brazil.

- Some other countries from Europe, Latin America and Asia, to add perspective.

The final composition of the group of interviewees is: France (6 interviews), the Netherlands (5), Spain (6), Italy (4), Great Britain (2), China (2), Taiwan (2), United States (9), Brazil (8), and 1 each from Russia, Hungary, Mexico,

Venezuela, Chile, Colombia, Paraguay, Aruba, Uruguay, South Korea, India, Japan.

Before living in Argentina, the interviewees also lived in countries other than their countries of origin: Germany, Australia, Belgium, Bosnia-Herzegovina, Brazil, Bulgaria, Canada, Colombia, China, Czech Republic, Ecuador, Egypt, France, Guatemala, Guinea, Hong Kong, Indonesia, Italy, Japan, Malaysia, Mexico, the Netherlands, Nigeria, Panama, Peru, Poland, Republic of the Congo, Rumania, Russia, Singapore, Slovakia, South Africa, Spain, Switzerland, Tunisia, Turkmenistan, Ukraine, United Kingdom, United States, Uruguay, Venezuela and Vietnam.

Throughout this book, quotes from the people interviewed are in italics. Next to each quote, I indicate between brackets their gender, country of origin and time spent in Argentina.

The interview

The questionnaire was made up of fourteen standardized questions, all of them open, which allowed people to respond what they wanted, spontaneously.

They were conducted by Hanneke Vaanhold (a Dutch journalist who has lived in Argentina for the past 12 years) and myself, using the native language of the interviewed person whenever it was possible, and when it wasn't, we used the language that was more comfortable for them: English, French or Spanish.

The period spanned May 2013 to June 2014.

1 : The image of the Argentine exists and it's unique

Before tackling this book, I asked myself if there was, in fact, a more or less homogeneous image of the Argentine. As you know (and as I, myself, learned), 100 years ago half of Buenos Aires' population was made up of immigrants arrived by sea, mostly from Spain, Italy, France, England and Ireland.

In the capital of Argentina, half of the population had been born abroad. That is why when walking through its streets you could see a French tramway foreman riding a horse, an Italian street vendor, an Asturian salesman, a Neapolitan organ player, a Galician woman servant and Turkish women wearing strange babuchas on their feet [...] Eating in a restaurant reminded you of the biblical Babel, clients and waiters came from all nations and the menu was barely decipherable gibberish. (La Argentina: historia del país y de su gente, María Sáenz Quesada)

The fundamental aim of the 1912 law [male, universal, secret and compulsory vote] was to build a national society, formed by citizens and not an agglomeration of natives, foreigners and sons of immigrants.

The Constitution of 1853 had been a first positive step; the common education act of 1884 was the second big step. (ibid)[3]

I am very impressed by the unique history of this immigration: the population of Buenos Aires tripled between 1850 and 1870 and then doubled between 1870 and 1914. I have trouble imagining scenes from that time. I think of the enormous effort that rulers and citizens alike had to make in order to adapt and assimilate. Although I almost never lived in the Netherlands, I carry in me the collective struggle of my people against the sea: for the Dutch, it was all about protecting themselves from the water and gaining ground on it[4]. I imagine that what Argentines carry in them is the idea of alienness.

How would this heterogeneity impact the results of my survey? Would the interviewees be able to play back an image of "the Argentines" or would their views all differ from one another? Would it be possible to establish similarities or is there still too much disparity and nothing to define the Argentine as such? Fortunately, the analysis of the interviews revealed very consistent perceptions as to the Argentine way of being. What a relief! The first result of my quest for theory was that there could be a theory. The image of the Argentine exists and it is unique.

"They are very Italian, the first big mistake a Spaniard makes is believing they are like us..." (man, Spain, 2 years)

---

[3] Quotes translated by Kist
[4] Today 26% of Dutch territory is below sea level and only about 50% of its land rises one metre or more above sea level.

"Argentines are quite similar to the Spanish, but they are more dramatic. Either they are the champions of the world or they are the worst thing on Earth: there is never a happy medium." (woman, Spain, 13 years)

"The Argentine is livelier than the Spaniard, much more awake". (man, Spain, 15 months)

"The Italians are more formal: they dress before they go out. Here, people go out the way they are, they care less about what others think". (woman, Italy, 3 years)

"Argentines are a lot messier, and more chaotic, than the Italians. They are warmer. They are more melancholic: everything is a problem; they always need to find something to cry about." (man, Italy, 2 years)

"Argentines are more Latin than we are." (man, France, 1 year)

"Their mentality is closer to the European one if you compare them with other Latin-American countries" (woman, Venezuela, 20 months)

"They are very open people, much more than Chileans" (woman, Chile, 6 years)

Personally, I will stick with the opinion that Fiona Adam expressed in *Culture shock Argentina: A Survival Guide to Customs & Etiquette*: "The country is a nation of immigrants who have generated a fiery blend of European sophistication and Latin passion in the heart of South America".

2 : Argentines are particularly friendly and welcoming (and good looking!)

The answers provided by my interviewees give me the impression that the people they are describing are the nicest in the world... Argentina is a country full of human warmth: Argentines are "kind", "warm", "welcoming"... they say.

I myself can testify: when my husband and I came to live here, his family and friends welcomed me as if they had known me forever. They included me at once. I never felt anything like *what-do-we-do-with-this-stranger-who-talks-funny*. My sisters-in-law gave me the keys to daily life (from bookstores to grocery stores), helped me find ballet lessons, activities for the kids and, on top of that, called often to see how I was adapting! My husband's friends patiently explained how things worked here. Maybe they sometimes laugh about my accent when my back is turned, but I really feel that they care about me.

And it looks like I am not alone:

"I am living a very good experience here, especially after living in England and Australia. People are warm, they try to understand you and help you." (woman, Brazil, 4 months)

"This is a friendly helpful nation" (woman, UK, 4 months)

"Everyone has Italian relatives and they make you feel comfortable. In Italy people treat foreigners as aliens." (woman, Italy, 3 years)

"While I was still living in Madrid, I did not have a favorable impression of Argentines. I saw them as excessively selfish, proud and calculating people. But when I came here I had no problems at all." (woman, Spain, 2 years)

They welcome you, even when they've never seen you before, and make you feel like they've known you your entire life." (man, Spain, 4 years)

"Great people, much more social than us." (man, Paraguay, 2 years)

"They smile immediately." (man, Netherlands, 5 months)

"More open to non-native speakers than in my past experiences, friendlier, more tolerant." (man, United States, 6 months)

"Very welcoming, very social, there's always time to drink some mate, have some facturas…" (man, United States, 6 years)

"They help others with their emotional needs. They offer you sympathy, a shoulder to cry on." (woman, Japan, 14 years)

"I had heard so many horrible stories about Argentines, I came with very low expectations. But Argentines are really friendly people." (woman, France, 2 months)

"When I first got here, my first reaction was one of surprise. I had a business partner in Brazil who never wanted to travel to Argentina or even hear about Argentines… I had this image of arrogant people. But I was surprised, because the first Argentines we met took SUCH good care of us, they really worried about us. (man, Brazil, 7 months)

This last quote reminds me of something a cab driver in Mexico told me not so long ago. He confessed that he didn't like Argentines because they were too self-important and that, when he saw potential clients from Argentina, he tried to direct them to another cab!

What on earth happens to Argentines when they travel? Why do they turn into other people?

They themselves even say they feel ashamed when they come across fellow countrymen outside of Argentina... I find this Argentine habit very strange: acting worse than they actually are, self-reinforcing their poor image.

But let's get back to the pleasant Argentine, the Argentine who isn't traveling :)

The kissing habit is one of the most obvious expressions of my theory #2. Argentines kiss a lot and it keeps surprising me: kissing, to me, is a rather intimate act which you save for the people you know well. Nevertheless, I try to get used to it and remind myself to greet everyone, every day, in every situation, with a kiss. Each time I forget to do so, I feel as if I have unintentionally provoked a major diplomatic incident, that usually only dissolves once the other person notices or remembers I am a foreigner. The most challenging are events with lots of people: I kiss, kiss and kiss without knowing who I am kissing, while wondering why so much intimacy is needed with people whom I will likely never see again. (Although I must admit that giving everybody a kiss is easier than having to think for each person, "this one deserves a handshake", "this one I have to kiss on the cheek", "nothing for this one"...).

Annabel from Holland recalls

The day I landed on Argentinean soil, I was holding my three-week old, first-born baby in my arms. The pediatrician in Holland had assured me that, since the baby had already regained his birth weight, it was OK to take the 15-hour long trip to Argentina with him, so we could reunite with his dad. That appointment probably took less than five minutes. The Dutch pediatrician seemed efficient, but somewhat distant: exactly what one expects from Dutch doctors toward their patients.

During my first weeks in Buenos Aires, what surprised me the most was the number of smiles and kind words on the street, in the supermarket, at the park: "How old is your baby? He's so cute, look at those eyes, he's huge", Argentines of all ages would say, spontaneously and without knowing me. Even a group of teenage boys once leaned over the baby carriage, a gesture which would be unthinkable among their peers in Northern Europe. The genuine attention made me feel good. As a new mom, I felt lonely and worried about the baby, whom I found adorable but very whiny. On top of that, he didn't seem to be growing, in spite of the innumerable breast feedings day and night.

Then, one afternoon I arrived at a recommended pediatrician's office. There were lots of people in the waiting-room, with their kids. Less than five minutes had passed when they called my name. Not one parent complained: they all looked at me patiently because my baby was a newborn. I stepped inside the examination room and put the baby seat on the floor. I was about to extend my hand when, unexpectedly, the pediatrician greeted me with a kiss, invited me to sit down and we started to talk. He asked me about Holland and expressed his admiration for Dutch painters, the beauty of tulip fields, the skills displayed by Holland's female hockey players in their last game against the national Leonas, and for a very nice Dutch person with whom he sailed every weekend...

Meanwhile, I felt guiltier every minute towards all the people waiting outside the door, losing their valuable time because of me. But the friendly conversation and human connection were actually distracting me from my problems for the first time since the baby's birth. I told the pediatrician about the baby's crying and his weight, and the scale confirmed my suspicions: he had only put on a few grams in the last two weeks. I started to feel down again. Slowly and carefully, the pediatrician completed the check-up. "Don't worry", he said and smiled in a reassuring way, "your baby is growing, both his height and his head, he is alert and completely healthy. The weight problem has a solution: you should rest more and worry less. Here is my house number: call me anytime you want." He sent me off with a kiss and a last pat on the back.

I exited his office completely renewed, fully endorsing my role as a confident mother. And this is only the first of a long sequence of situations that caught my attention during my years in Argentina and which demonstrate the extraordinary warmth of these people, which I consider to be the possible solution to many problems, big and small.

"They kiss much more than we do, men kiss each other – that's weird." (woman, Brazil, 2 years)

"Doctors kiss you on the cheek here! And my doctor patted my back. I blushed because he was really handsome!" (woman, France, 1 year)

"I used to work with 30 people. I had to kiss each of these 30 people each morning, I had no choice. There was a Russian girl who didn't do it. She was not well liked at all." (woman, Spain, 4 years)

"Everyone kisses everyone and men kiss too! It's awkward. I read that they started the kiss thing 20 years ago as a way to make the country more friendly" (woman, US, 17 months)

"They kiss everybody. Coming from a bowing country, it is quite a culture shock." (woman, India, 2 years)

Beyond the kissing, Argentines are also generally much more effusive than other nationalities.

"Argentines are demonstrative, and Asians aren't. We Easterners never know if we are loved [by our parents]: we can't feel it, can't see it. One day, a Canadian friend told me "I don't know what's with Asian guys, you never know what they're feeling… I want to start dating Western guys again". (woman, Taiwan, 15+ years)

It turns out Argentines are not only pleasant on a social level, but also on a physical one, and they have a unique style. Before moving here, I remember I was always positively impressed by their unique sense of appearance. Children's clothes for example: I always bought them during our visits to Buenos Aires because they were much more elegant than in the United States, and trendier than European kids' apparel.

"Argentine men are very handsome. They are a mix that I like. They're beautiful people." (woman, France, 1 year)

"Argentine girls take more care of their appearance than Spanish ones." (man, Spain, 15 months)

"Nice attitude, and they dress well." (man, Russia, 11 years)

"I like the fashion here, they look good, they exercise, they are trendy …" (man, United States, 6 months)

"I like the men's long hair! And the women's hair is long and straight and always gorgeous." (woman, United States, 17 months)

"They have a messy, yet trendy look. That is something of their own, not so Americanized". (woman, Venezuela, 20 months)

"Very well dressed, always wearing perfume, it suits them. I see it as a European thing, to be well-dressed. In Brazil we are less formal" (woman, Brazil, 7 months)

"Argentine girls are pretty. Many of them are." (man, Taiwan, 20 + years)

"Women are beautiful..." (man, United States, 8 years)

And the men are both charming and perfect gentlemen.

"Argentine men open the door for you. In Korea, that would never happen! Korean men are very strict with women: here they demonstrate love, over there they don't." (woman, Korea, 14 years)

The man from the poultry shop

A few days after arriving in Buenos Aires I went to buy chicken at a poultry shop (I had never seen a shop entirely dedicated to chicken in all its forms, so that in itself was already an exciting experience). I entered the store and walked towards the counter. After a moment, an employee called out "54". Only then did I realize I had to take a number from the dispenser at the entrance (the little paper number system is excellent, but it doesn't exist everywhere and it had been years since I'd last seen it). I walked up to the machine.

At that point, a very Argentine-looking elderly gentleman, who seemed to be coming straight out of a milonga, had just entered and pulled a number. He saw I was distressed... and handed me his little piece of paper! In many other places, he would have taken pleasure in being helped before me.

From time to time however, the Argentine suffers a true metamorphosis. A Frenchman interviewed for this book expressed it perfectly: *"The Argentine in his car isn't the same person as outside of it. He can stand in line inside a bank for hours, but in his car he always has to go first. The street is his."*

"What I can't stand is the impatience on the street, I don't understand it." (woman, France, 7 years)

"In the automobile they can be pretty rude, very selfish drivers – they don't stop for pedestrians. You are as good as dead if you don't look very well. I have never seen drivers as selfish and rude/obnoxious as here!" (man, United States, 6 months)

"Too much disorder compared to Russia: the way they drive, they overtake cars anywhere they can". (man, Russia, 11 years)

"They have an ego-problem. Look at the way they drive!" (man, Italy, 7 years)

"I'm worried about getting hit by a bus or a car, having an accident because of the crazy driving." (woman, United States, 17 months)

When I first got here, I was afraid to use the car. Then, little by little, I started with short rides, which I progressively extended, like a cat getting used to a new house. Every time I came back home, I felt as if I had just completed an obstacle course and needed a drink (or two). Never in my 33 years as a driver had I seen so much passion for shortcuts, so much turning without signals (how am I supposed to know where the Argentine person in front of me is going?), so much lane changing to gain a fraction of a second, so many violations of yellow lines, so many right turns from left lanes, so many cars pulling out of narrow streets and claiming right-of-way, or so many hazard lights flashing while driving as if to say I-will-be-doing-something-very-strange-at-some-point-not-sure-exactly-when-but-watch-out!

Where did the pleasant, welcoming and friendly Argentine go?

3 : Argentines talk a lot

The monetary inflation in Latin America is a serious problem, but the inflation of words is as bad as the inflation of currency, if not worse; there is a terrible excess of supply. (Eduardo Galeano)[5].

"This is a nation that loves to talk and will do so loudly at every available opportunity." (Fiona Adams in Cultureshock Argentina: A Survival Guide to Customs & Etiquette)

Reading the above sentences encouraged me to write this little theory. I too believe that Argentines talk a lot and, what is even worse (for foreigners), they use a lot of words and say everything so fast! According to a study from the University of Lyon (France), a Spanish speaker pronounces in average 7.83 syllables per second, compared to 7.18 for a French speaker and 6.19 for an English speaker.

"They are quite direct people (I enjoy this) who like to talk." (man from Holland, 2 years in Argentina)

---

[5] Quote translated by Kist

"They are happy to talk to you, despite the language barrier. Once you start talking they talk forever." (woman, China, 4 months)

"Good oratory skills, they have extensive vocabulary, know how to speak in public." (man, Spain, 2 years)

Their pronunciation is beautiful (especially when they make a lot of rolled "r "sounds), and listening to Argentines speak enthusiastically can be astounding (God, when do they breathe?). I also admire the use of the past-perfect-subjunctive tense, so elegant and distinguished. But, for foreigners, the combination of a long speech, with so many words pronounced so fast can become a deadly cocktail. I would guess that quite a few foreigners (that's my case at least) only understand about 33% of what they hear. Whenever an Argentine speaks to me in this fast rhythm, I feel as if I were inside a wave that is dragging me without anything to hold onto. The person starts, I begin to feel lost, more and more lost, and suddenly I wonder whether the other person has noticed that I am drowning. The feeling only goes away when the person stops talking. And only then do I gather the courage to ask them to start all over again, but slower please this time.

Something similar happens with written language: sentences are long and extremely abundant in words. Sometimes I feel that reading in Spanish is like a treasure hunt: you have to find the hidden meaning between so many words.

In my former workplace, I used to pour myself a cup of coffee each time I got an email from an Argentine colleague, because I knew it would be lo-o-o-ng. Not to mention the official documents (legal, contractual or administrative), which seem to be written in a separate language, a secret code only comprehensible to people who have passed some inaccessible initiation rite. For instance, this is what I find on the welcome (!) page of my bank:

Por disposición del BCRA (Com. "A" 4895) las Entidades Financieras deberán identificar a los clientes que se encuentran incluidos dentro de la categoría de "Personas Expuestas Políticamente" (Peps) y solicitarles de considerarlo necesario información adicional. Revisten la calidad de Peps las personas incluidas en el punto 1.3.4.3. de la citada comunicación. El texto de la referida norma se encuentra disponible en www.bcra.gov.ar pudiendo ser consultado en Normativa / Comunicaciones. Aquellos clientes que, por alguna de las circunstancias que se exponen en la normativa descripta precedentemente, cumplan con esta condición deberán notificarlo en la sucursal correspondiente.

According to the BCRA (Communication "A" 4895), financial entities should identify clients that are included in the category of "Politically Exposed Persons" (Peps) and ask them for additional information if deemed necessary. Are considered responding to the quality of Peps people included in point 1.3.4.3. of the abovementioned communication. The text of the referred norm is available at www.bcra.gov.ar and can be consulted in Normative / Communications. Those customers who, due to any of the circumstances described in the regulation described above, comply with this condition must notify it in the corresponding branch.

At the same time, the social aspect of Argentines' verbal inflation has something very charming.

Expressions like "¿viste?"[6], "¿entendés?"[7] or "mirá vos"[8], which are typically Argentine, are friendly manners of addressing the other, of including him or her in the conversation.

"I love the fact that anyone in the street just talks to you." (woman, Chile, 6 years)

"In France you could be at a café for 4 hours without talking to anyone; here there will necessarily be an interaction... Encounters are more fluid, spontaneous." (woman, France, 6 months)

"They LOVE to talk – the dinners can last very long and they don't drink that much alcohol. Still, the conversation is fun". (man, United States, 17 months)

"They are naturally fun without alcohol. They don't need to get drunk to have a good time – Americans drink a lot". (woman, United States, 17 months)

---

[6] Literally "you see?" Argentines frequently use this rhetorical question after a sentence or statement to seek acknowledgement from the listener, thus creating an implicit bond with that person (similar to "you know" in English).

[7] Literally "you understand?" Argentines use it in a rhetorical way at the end of a sentence or statement to make sure the other person fully grasps what is being said and to seek their approval or acknowledgement.

[8] Literally "look at you". Argentines use it to reply to something the other has said, either to express awe ("wow, look at you!") or surprise/interest ("really? Is that right?").

"Chinese people could learn [from the Argentines] to open themselves a bit more, to speak to others. Asians are very reserved, they don't speak easily". (man, Taiwan, 20+ years)

"In my family in Taiwan, when we're finished eating everyone goes to their room. Here, we stay at the table and talk for an hour and a half." (woman, Taiwan, 15+ years)

"Paraguayans could learn [from the Argentines] to talk more in order to exteriorize their feelings and not always put up with everything." (man, Paraguay, 2 years)

"In my country they say 'hello', here they say 'hi, how are you?' and they truly want to know how you are doing! In Russia you only ask this to intimate people, friends." (man, Russia, 11 years)

And then there is their particular version of Spanish, with the yeísmo[9] and voseo[10], the lunfardo[11] and some terms that only Argentines know precisely how to use.

---

[9] In most parts of Argentina and Uruguay, letters <ll> and <y> are pronounced /ʒ/ (like the sound of "si" in "delusion"), instead of the classical /ʎ/ (like the "y" in "yellow"). In Buenos Aires, especially among younger generations, the /ʒ/ sound has evolved into /ʃ/ ("shh").

[10] In Argentina and Uruguay, when referring to somebody in 2nd person, people use the pronoun "vos" instead of "tú".

[11] Originally a slang used by the lower and lower-middle classes of Buenos Aires and Montevideo in the late 19th and early 20th century, many of the Lunfardo vocabulary and phrases have become part of common language in Argentina and Uruguay.

When I visited Argentina in 2001, for instance, I was 6-months pregnant. Every person I met, acquaintances as well as strangers, said *"¡estás bárbara!"* (literally, 'you are barbarous!'). And I always felt offended because I thought it was a negative thing to say, describing me as a sort of inhumane creature, a barbarian (which, at the same time, is exactly how you feel when you're pregnant). It took me a while to realize that it was actually something positive, a compliment, and that the same word was commonly used in many other situations to mean "great".

"I learned Spanish in Spain. Here, in the beginning it was hard to understand people and nobody understood me either. I asked for a street called Lavalle (without pronouncing it "Lavasshe") and no one knew what I was talking about." (woman, France, 6 months)

"I love how Argentine girls speak" (man, Spain, 15 months)

"They have typical words: 'espectacular', 'bárbaro', 'no te puedo creer', '¡ah mirá!', '¡mirá vos!'" (woman, Spain, 18 months)

Personally, I love the Argentines' histrionics, that habit of exaggerating and intensifying each statement. "It's *tremendously* cold", for instance, when it is only 10°C. Or the idea of the "sensación térmica" (windchill factor), making the real temperature seem even colder.

I find some expressions absolutely genius, like for instance "*se traspapeló*" (when a document has been

32

"mislaid"), or "*se me complicó el día*" ("my day got complicated", a very polite excuse), or "*tengo que hacer un trámite*" (I have a formality to take care of, in other words, something-important-to-do-that-will-take-an-indefinite-amount-of-time-and-requires-your-fullest-patience-because-I'll-be-late).

In a country with such a high level of verbosity, there still remains one area of speech however where less seems to be more. And that is the question of names. I find it strange that no one here uses their full name, and that instead they call each other with short versions of their names or nicknames. They love nicknames: Sandy, Ale, Nacho, Lu, Pancho, Andre… One day, in ballet class, my teacher asked me my name. "Martina", I said. She immediately asked me: "And how do they call you?" Somewhat hesitant and shy, I said: "Uhhhh…. Martina". (She never spoke to me again). I believe that Sandra, Alejandro, Ignacio, Lucía, Francisco, Andrea are prettier, more important and even more Argentine-sounding names than the corresponding nicknames. As for me, please never call me "Martu"!

Of course, everything has its flip side, and among the interviewees many believe that Argentine verbosity is unnecessary. This reminds me of a Swedish joke. One friend asks the other: "Want to go for a drink?" "Let's go", says the other, and they go to a bar. They order aquavit. Before they drink, the first one inquires: "How are you?" "Fine", replies the other. And they both empty their glass in a single shot. They order a second one. Before they drink, the first man asks his friend: "How about your wife?" "Fine", says the other and they empty their glass in one shot again. They get a third one. Before they drink, the first one asks: "And your family?" And the other replies dryly: "Listen, friend, did we come here to drink or to talk?"

"They make a lot of fuss over nothing." (woman, Holland, 5 years)

"They are raucous, boisterous." (man, United States, 6 years)

"I acquired my work culture in the US. When I had a business meeting there it was 1, 2, 3 problems and a solution. Dealing with Argentines is very different. You need to become friends first. Then, you exchange small-talk and anecdotes for three hours and before you know it the meeting is over, and you haven't talked business at all." (man, Spain, 4 years)

"They don't let people speak. They speak over each other's voice in a louder tone, that's their way of taking the floor. In a business meeting with 15 people, it is shouting over shouting over shouting. They should listen to each other more, respect and learn from other opinions." (woman, Venezuela, 20 months)

"Charlatans. You ask one question about anything and it turns out they have a PhD on the topic..." (man, France, 15 years)

"They are charlatans, they talk incessantly, and sometimes they talk a lot without saying anything." (man, Taiwan, 20+ years)

Li-Mei from China recalls

When I went to the first mothers' meeting at my son's school it felt like being at the epicenter of pandemonium. The mothers were supposed to address three topics but ended up discussing the same one for two hours. They gesticulated, shouted, and continuously interrupted each other. The words I heard most during the meeting were "hey! wait a minute" with the hand signal that went along with it, while the mother who was speaking had to stand up and shout to repeat her opinion again and again. I might be wrong, but I think they enjoyed it. They never reached an agreement. How terribly inefficient, I unintentionally thought, feeling dazed.

I used to take a walk with my dog every day in my neighborhood. Unknown passersby always greeted me. In the supermarket, the grocery store or the bakery, people treated me so well that each time I stayed inside a while longer. The day my mom came to visit me from China, I took her on my usual walk around the neighborhood: supermarket, grocery store and bakery. The baker asked me about my vacation. While I was answering, I suddenly heard my mother sigh impatiently. "What's wrong?" I asked. "We aren't getting anywhere! You keep stopping and speaking to everyone. Hurry up!" she replied. She was right. But it was only then that I realized how much I enjoyed these inefficient but oh-how-lovely encounters that you only get in Argentina.

Another fact about Argentines is they are quite foul-mouthed. And for foreigners, it can be confusing to realize that the same words used to insult each other are also used in situations of camaraderie. An Argentine friend explains this very well: "Bad words have multiple interpretations here whereas in other countries, they only have one meaning."

Many foreigners luckily don't understand the bad words, but native Spanish-speakers are more sensitive to them.

"They speak badly to each other but that's part of the way they are: they are very expressive and vulgar: "pelotudo, que hacés, hijo de puta" [asshole, what's up son of a bitch]. When I first arrived I found it very rude." (man, Colombia, 4 years)

"How rude they can be – their vocabulary, the bad words – with strangers and in front of their kids. I am happy my kids don't understand Spanish, sometimes it's embarrassing." (woman, Aruba, 9 months)

"Rudeness is typically Argentine. Bad words are a natural part of their language… That's what two bosses told me, one from Uruguay and one from Spain: they say a lot of bad words, but that's part of the way they are. If you say the same thing in Paraguay you make a really bad impression…" (man, Paraguay, 2 years)

"You can see it in the way they drive… They don't care whether you're a woman, they call you "pelotuda"[12]. They called me all kinds of things. Mexican drivers, when they see you're a woman, they control themselves." (woman, Mexico, 4 years)

The other day, in front of my house, a 5-year-old boy was riding his bike with training wheels alongside his mother. "*Boludo, boludo, boludo*" (jerk, jerk, jerk), he kept on shouting. And the mother didn't say anything.

---

[12] This common adjective in Argentina can mean all sorts of things: "stupid", "jerk", "asshole", "useless"…

4 : Argentines are everyday superheroes

When I arrived in Argentina, I took interest in the country's history. This society has gone through a lot: the hardships of the first settlers, the long wait for ships from Spain, violent government changes, dictatorships, cyclical economic crises... A true rollercoaster for which the locals are well-prepared, but which completely surprises foreigners.

Argentines are "resilient" and "invincible" superheroes. They are incredibly creative as far as survival is concerned.

"I admire their patience; I wouldn't be capable of that kind of strength. On the social and political level, any sort of "shit" happens: they accept it and start over again. Like during the 2001 crisis: we'll just put our money someplace else... they always find individual solutions. When there's a problem, it's all right, life goes on." (woman, France, 7 years)

"If it doesn't work one way, they try another way, and they only stop in front of something forbidden. What capacity for adaptation!" (woman, France, 1 year)

"When they fall, they start over." (man, Taiwan 20 years)

"They have a certain optimism which, when things go wrong, enables them to rise above the situation. They let the storm pass and try to make things better. They don't sink along with the ship." (man, France, 1 year)

"When Argentines decide to go live in another country they often do very well: if you can manage to survive here, you can make it anywhere." (man, Holland, 2 years)

"They are smart and creative businessmen." (man, Italy, 7 years)

"They're very innovative. It's a dynamic society." (woman, Uruguay, 6 years)

That's probably why, in the face of a situation which personally would take me to the limit of my patience, Argentines are usually pretty relaxed. "It's as if they were made out of rubber", a Russian interviewee perfectly described. "You stretch, stretch, and they don't break. I would already have exploded".

"Frenchmen would jump off the Eiffel Tower if they were confronted with the 2001 Argentina crisis... Argentines know how to swim in troubled waters." (man, France, 15 years)

"In Holland everything is planned in advance: if you want to see someone you have to schedule it three weeks in advance." (woman, Holland, 4 years)

Ricardo from Brazil recalls

I've been in this country for a year. I arrived on a sailboat from Sao Paolo and I live on it with my family, in a boat club, surrounded by Argentines who love sailing. The other day I had a problem with the device I use to measure the wind. I feared having to buy another one (the device costs around $11.000!).

But one of the Argentines from the club told me he was going to give me the full device for free. And he did. He gave me a little strip of cloth that costs about $6 and that solves the problem: it measures the direction of the wind and tells you whether it is strong or not. Sure, it doesn't tell you the exact intensity of the wind, but "why do you need to know the exact intensity of the wind anyway?" he asked me. "It only influences you psychologically..." And he was right.

Argentines look for simple solutions, more practical and cheaper. Why would you make everything more complicated? I see great strength there.

"One day I wanted to watch a soccer game and my (Argentine) girlfriend had invited 30 people over for a party. It didn't bother her at all: she just called all the 30 people and told them the party would be the next day."
(man, Holland, 2 years)

"If they have a problem, they don't sweat it. Whenever I need to cancel something or am unable to go somewhere, people adapt. In Europe, it would be the end of the world, people feel you're making their lives more complicated!" (woman, Spain, 2 years)

"Family relations in Argentina are very different from the WASP culture where even with your most intimate family members get-togethers are always scheduled, planned... Here there is much more social flexibility and people are happy when a family member shows up, it's not a big deal." (man, United States, 6 years)

"My Argentine family makes fun of me because I like to plan: They always ask me "So, what are we going to plan now?" (woman, United States, 2 years)

I admit that for someone like me, who has neither the Argentine resilience nor their experience, things can be a bit harder. In the twelve months since my arrival [in February 2013], not only did I have to take on all sorts of new challenges on a personal level, but I also had to learn about the official dollar vs. the blue dollar, the green dollar and the tourist dollar; I had to get used to high inflation, subsidized prices and shortage of certain products; to the significant discounts when you pay with this or that bank's credit card, the smaller discounts when you pay in cash, to trains without a schedule, to "A-receipts" vs. the "common receipts" in stores, not to mention the effort involved in knowing on which day I should use which card in which supermarket or with which dollar-rate I should convert the price of an item...

Until one day, when I finally thought I had it under control, the cashier asked me: "en cuotas?" *(in installments?)*. And then, it started all over again: the confusion, the math (interests and inflation vs. cash), and the feeling that I would never, ever, understand how it all works. (Although I admit I have found a few strategies for situations when I am unsure what to do: the first one consists in saying "yes" with a big smile when asked to choose between 2 options – knowing the other person will end up picking the more logical one when they realize I don't understand anything –, and the second is to say that I want whatever most people choose. Ha!)

"People are really smart here, they calculate extremely fast". (man, Holland, 15 years)

"They have great financial skills, the delivery boy knows more about finance than I do." (man, Spain, 2 years)

I also remember the first time I was asked to give my ID number in the supermarket. One item more on this long list of disorientation: common receipt? cash or card? ID number, please. Help! I had never been asked to give an ID number in public. Sometimes I was asked to show identification (called "document" in Argentina), but never to say the number aloud and by heart. One of my Dutch interviewees described this feeling very well: in Argentina, it's as if you are "guilty until proven innocent".

Just like me, every person I interviewed has experienced his or her own daily obstacle course and, leaving aside the language, the following are the most common barriers they face.

43

The limited offer of products

"I don't find the same products all the time in the supermarket – the offer is unstable, it's strange. This doesn't happen in Brazil, didn't happen in Russia – so I hoard food now". (woman, Brazil, 2 years)

"Variety is lacking in certain products compared to other places in the world. Also, the price of electronics is ridiculous because of protectionism…." (man, United States, 6 years)

"I've become a hoarder!" (woman, India, 2 years)

Bureaucracy

"I had to go to the courtroom three days in a row to get my car back after it was taken by the tow truck. Other foreigners I know had similar experiences." (woman, France, 1 year)

"Bureaucracy, paperwork, everything takes a lot of time. The mail: you can't get packages, either they never arrive or you have to go fetch them someplace far". (woman, Spain, 2 years)

"Bureaucracy, paperwork, documents, signatures, stamps…" (man, Brazil, 2 years)

"There are new bureaucratic rules every month: for federal taxes, the bank…" (woman, India, 2 years)

"Chinese people don't travel to Argentina for tourism

because it's very complicated to get a visa (and it's far!). It's easier for us to get a visa for the US than one for Argentina, which takes months and requires many more documents." (man, China, 2 years)

Financial difficulties

"It's hard to build a future here, there's more economic stress, more problems... It reduces your independence." (man, Holland, 2 years)

"We earn in pesos and lose a lot of money because of the official exchange rate." (man, Brazil, 7 months)

"The feeling of economic uncertainty. I feel good here, I'm happy with my work and my income but there's the fear of the Argentine peso. Everyone tells you to buy dollars. You're never sure what to do. There's no way to plan: if you start saving pesos, you feel you're losing money." (man, Colombia, 4 years)

Everyday unpredictability

"There are too many surprises with the administration: trains stop service, buses stop service, people stop traffic... In China we have one party, not so much administration. Demonstrations aren't allowed and even if they were, people wouldn't demonstrate because they listen to the government" (man, China, 2 years)

"The transportation. Whether by car, bus, subway or plane: you never know how long it'll take you to go from point A to point B. The power outages." (man, France, 1 year)

"Chaos, uncertainty about when things will start/end. In Mexico we got our foreigner documents within 3 months, here there's always a problem..." (woman, Uruguay, 6 years)

Actually, the day-to-day problems in Argentina distract from – but also reflect - bigger problems, which are obvious from my outside perspective and that of the interviewees. I am referring to corruption, inflation, physical and economic insecurity, lack of trust in institutions, economic inequality and unequal opportunities. And there is real danger here, because the great enemy of heroes is known to be complacency: "In Latin America we specialize in waiting for our *deus ex machina* [...] an Olympic divinity that will save everyone from their problems." (Leila Marcor -a Venezuelan living in Uruguay-, *Lamentablemente estamos bien*, Bolsillo Editions)

"They are not very ambitious." (man, Holland, 5 months)

"The problem is that the Argentine always adapts to the situation. An Argentine told me that!" (woman, Taiwan, 15+ years)

"What bothers me is that they don't take action. When products are scarce, they whine but they don't do anything." (woman, France, 7 years)

"For such a wealthy country in terms of culture, minds, land, oil, they have so much to offer and the current political situation stifles their growth and their image on a global level." (woman, United States, 2 years)

"They even boycott their own projects. They don't try to unite to emerge from this situation. Instead of that, they blame each other or say they will never make it, no, no, no…" (woman, Uruguay, 6 years)

"They've got to stop psychoanalyzing themselves and start doing something." (man, Italy, 3 years)

My dear Argentine superheroes: as Spiderman's uncle once said (and before him, Voltaire): with great strength comes great responsibility. What if you saved some of that strength to start fixing some issues?

5 : Argentines are faithful

I can already imagine the face of some of my interviewees when they read the title of this chapter. They'll probably be thinking it's the exact opposite of what they said!

"Faithfulness doesn't exist here. The normal thing is to have a wife and a mistress, or a husband and a lover." (man, Spain, 15 months)

"I hear about many situations of infidelity. It's a little strange that in a country as Catholic as Argentina, people are so unfaithful and they actually admit it!" (man, Holland, 2 years)

"In this culture there is a lot of cheating…" (woman, United Kingdom, 3 years)

"They are very family oriented, but I also heard they cheat a lot – which is a paradox." (woman, Brazil, 2 years)

Actually, my theory has nothing to do with faithfulness in romantic relationships (I'm afraid no country is perfect in this area). The faithfulness I want to address here is the loyalty toward family and friends, a typically Argentine devotion.

It doesn't really matter whether it is because of their Italian roots or the hardships they encountered as a society, the truth is: relations between Argentines and their family and friends are amazing, and almost all of the people I interviewed have mentioned this.

"Family values are very important. In my opinion the Sunday "asado[13]" is something very positive." (man, Holland, 2 years)

"We could learn to make more time for family, to treat family as something more important. In Holland elderly people are placed in a nursing home and get visits from their relatives once a month." (woman, Holland, 4 years)

"Family here is fundamental. Friendship ties are stronger than in Spain." (woman, Spain, 2 years)

"Argentines are very family-oriented, it must be their Italian roots. They spend the weekends and holidays with their family, even New Year's Eve. Family always comes first, and I am talking about the WHOLE family, not only the direct family." (woman, United Kingdom, 3 years)

"At restaurants you see three generations, large groups of extended family, lots of children, they value children, celebrate their children." (man, United States, 6 months)

---

[13] *Asado* refers to a traditional way of preparing grilled meat in Argentina, Chile, Paraguay and Uruguay (their equivalent of barbecue) but also more generally to the social event that surrounds it: *asados* can be seen as the pretext for gathering extended family and/or friends around the table (or rather around the grill) once a week, generally on Sunday.

"Here you see warm, big families, much more than in Hungary. Family is very important to them, the woman is the strong person in the family..." (woman, Hungary, 3 months)

"I love that family is really important – I like that they enjoy living with each other. I am always the first one to get up to clean, but the family says 'sit down, let's talk'." (woman, United States, 2 years)

"On Sundays, for asados, they spend 4 hours eating together!!" (man, United States, 8 years)

"Brazilians could learn to value family and social relations more. We Brazilians are happy all-day long but we don't invite you to our home." (woman, Brazil, 4 years)

"Sunday is the (extended) family day. They meet with their family to argue, have discussions. Sunday asado is never skipped. In Colombia it's not such a strong institution as it is here." (man, Colombia, 4 years)

"The value of friendship. You never treat a friend with disrespect. Friends are always there to help you." (woman, Italy, 3 years)

"They are very loyal to their family and their childhood friends." (woman, Holland, 5 years)

"In Europe, in Paris for example, most groups of friends will split after high school. Buenos Aires is a huge city too, but Argentines still hang out with their groups from high school." (woman, France, 2 months)

"I like Argentine traditions like asados and meeting up with friends." (woman, Mexico, 4 years)

"What most surprised me is the quality of the relationship, the capacity to actively form part of a group (not just occasionally). The group is intense, it is present in your life, and it gives you a sense of belonging." (woman, Spain, 3 years)

As for me, I don't have many friends here yet, but I notice that in the groups to which I do belong (the parents at my children's school, the students from ballet class) people take much more care of me than they used to in other places. It seems as though they are truly interested. Thank you for including me!

This character trait may surprise people from some countries, in a positive manner, but it can also be acquired (and taught):

"Whenever I can, I tell other Chinese parents [living in Argentina] about the importance of socializing. Because for Chinese people, the most important thing is the academic level." (woman, Taiwan, 30 years, interviewed in La Nación Revista, 07/28/13, on the topic "Argenchinos")

With all these comments in mind I asked myself about the difference between Argentines and other cultures in this particular area. Because family and friends exist in every country, sometimes even going a long way back (my parents, for instance, are over 75 and still meet once a year, in Holland, with their college friends).

What strikes me as peculiar in this country are the strong ties maintained through time with entire groups of friends that sometimes go all the way back to childhood. An Argentine woman in her forties once told me that she goes out once a month with her high school friends. I know this must seem very normal to the Argentine reading this, but it isn't. The value attributed to friendship and its associated traditions (big and frequent get-togethers) in this country is not that common in other latitudes.

"Family and friends are like a social pact" (woman, India, 2 years)

That's probably why, in the face of a situation which personally would take me to the limit of my patience, Argentines are usually pretty relaxed. "It's as if they were made out of rubber", a Russian interviewee perfectly described. "You stretch, stretch, and they don't break. I would already have exploded".

For foreigners who aren't used to this (or perhaps are jealous), always being with the same people can seem asphyxiating. Others believe that Argentines tend to stagnate with the same group and that this would explain why they don't open up to new and different ideas. Staying in their comfort zone would prevent them from experimenting the "spark of creativity" that stems from encounters with others.

Other people simply think it's a strategy to have an excuse ready to miss work: because "my sister-in-law is sick", for instance.

Maybe there's a bit of truth in all of this, but none of these interpretations will stop me from saying to the Argentines, loud and clear: YOU PEOPLE SURE HAVE YOUR PRIORITIES IN ORDER!

Aneko from Japan recalls

Ever since my first days in Argentina, I was surprised by how much support Argentines gave me, like for instance the real-estate lady who assisted me with the most tedious tasks – which weren't even part of her job – only so that I would feel more comfortable in my new destination.

In the following years, Argentines kept being very nice to me, but I had a hard time deepening that friendship. Until one day, while I was drinking tea with some friends, one of them realized I was feeling sad. She literally lent me her shoulder to cry on, took my hand and said the precise words I needed to comfort and soothe me.

This has happened to me lots of times since then: Argentines have extraordinary compassion and empathy. It's like an extra sense, they are the best friends. When they open their door to you, they are opening the door to their soul and you will never leave it.

6 : Argentines have a recipe for happiness

As an economist, I like to compare the state of affairs across the world. In this field, new indicators regularly come up and measuring "happiness" is one of them: this relatively new trend seeks to complete traditional per capita income data to better assess a society's well-being.

Basing herself on statistical research, Carol Graham, author of "*The pursuit of happiness*", states the following:

"Everywhere that I have studied happiness, some very simple patterns hold: a stable marriage, good health, and enough (but not too much) income are good for happiness. Unemployment, divorce, and economic instability are terrible for happiness."

"The one thing people have a hard time adapting to is uncertainty."

"The unhappy are most likely to migrate to seek better opportunities."

"Friendship and relatives mattered more to the well-being of the average Latin American respondent than health, employment or personal assets."

Based on the first three statements, a natural question arises: how on earth could Argentines be happy, subject as they are to their economy's chaotic movements and the uncertainty of everyday life, while the blood in their veins is that of unhappy ancestors who migrated in search of a better life? Would this explain their reputation of melancholic tango dancers? Yet the fourth consideration has to do with family and friends which are really important here... so how does it pan out?

Let's see. Argentines ranked 29th in the *World Happiness Report 2013*[14] (out of 156 countries, which places them in the "top 20%"). In comparison, they rank 55th (out of 187, thus "top 30%") in terms of per capita gross national income in 2013, according to the IMF's *World Economic Outlook Database 2014*.

Conclusion: Argentines are happier than they are rich.

What then, is their recipe?

In my view -and the interviewees will agree-, the secret lies in finding a fair (or happy) medium: a balance between work and personal life, between what is useful and what is enjoyable. That same balance which we have lost in some countries (provided we ever had it in the first place).

---

[14] Helliwell, John F., Richard Layard, and Jeffrey Sachs, eds. 2013. World Happiness Report 2013. New York: UN Sustainable Development Solutions Network, www.unsdsn.com.

For foreigners living in Argentina, this comes as quite a revelation: it *is* actually possible to take some time to live without the world coming to an end! How can that be? Is it no longer necessary to control every aspect of life, to be busy all the time?

Some months ago, I saw a play which setting was in a museum in Paris. Between each act, small groups of actors entered the scene pretending to be groups of tourists. There were the Japanese visitors, taking pictures every second; the teenagers, with their iPods and hoodies and a group of Dutch "tourists", dressed in orange. Their Dutch guide kept asking them to hurry because they still had lots of things to do: the bus was waiting to take them to the next museum, then to the Eiffel Tower, then to the boat which would carry them along the Seine and to the bus again to go to Montmartre for a dinner under the moonlight. They seemed somewhat distressed!

I must confess I am very much like that. Most of the time I carry a list of things to do in my head as well as a "master plan" for the next few years, which I always come back to and adjust as needed to make sure I don't divert from my general path. I used to think that everyone lived like this and that people got as nervous as I did when they weren't doing something completely productive towards the list or the plan.

But one day I moved to Mexico and eventually I landed in Argentina. Since then, I learned to leave a small space in my head for an item on the list that reads: "don't do anything and simply enjoy from time to time".

"Argentines are very happy people, they spend their time complaining but are actually very happy. Enjoying the moment is the best thing you can do." (woman, from Spain, 13 years in Argentina)

Catherine from France recalls

One day I met an Argentine man who asked me what plans I had for the weekend. Since we had just arrived and didn't have friends or family in town, he worried about us. I told him I planned to go shopping on Saturday to do some work around the house with my husband on Sunday.

He asked me – as a joke – if I was German and finally said I was mad: "Week-ends are for having an asado with friends and looking at the sky".

I love this aspect of Argentine people, this ability to sit down and enjoy the weather, take their time and savor a good moment. In France we cannot be inactive.

Most of the foreigners I interviewed have experienced the same revelation as me, albeit with variations according to the person and the nationality. For Brits, North Americans and Asians, the discovery is essentially that work and productivity aren't everything, and that their lives could actually be fuller if they learned to enjoy them more.

"People here work to play, they don't work to work. In the UK and the US, people are obsessed with work. It's the first thing they talk about in a conversation. ... They don't take time to enjoy life. Everything is about saving money." (woman, United Kingdom, 3 years)

"In restaurants here, everyone is so NOT in a hurry, people enjoy their meals, you don't get the check together with the hamburger, they don't show you out the door." (woman, United States, 17 months)

"[We could learn from the Argentines that...] If we learned to relax, our quality of life would go up. I don't know in which other country they have this balance and are able to realize work is not everything." (man, United States, 8 years)

"Here you can't find coffee to go because people sit down to have coffee – in the US people always have to rush, do things fast... they should take a chill pill, sit down for 10 minutes. Americans think they are the most productive – there has to be a sweet spot somewhere in the middle. Take the time to experience social moments" (man, United States, 6 years)

"We Americans have a work ethic that says, if you're not working 40+ hours a week and taking only 2 weeks off in the year, you aren't competitive – that's why we don't understand the world" (woman, United States, 6 months)

"I appreciate the balance they have been able to strike between work and play. They work hard but also leave time for enjoyments." (woman, United States, 2 months)

"They enjoy life (that's the big difference between US and Argentina). In the US, I work because that's what I'm about whereas in Argentina I work so I can enjoy the weekends and can have fun." (woman, United States, 2 years)

"In China we have a saying: you work hard the first half of your life and in the second half you spend everything on health. In China, a person's value is linked to their level of success, their house, their cars; everyone wants to have it all. It's not about happiness or feelings. In Argentina, if they have enough to live, they're happy." (man, China, 2 years)

"Japan has a very controlling system. Here we can learn to relax and enjoy life, not go through life too competitive and worrying." (woman, Japan, 14 years)

For Continental Europeans, the revelation is that they don't have to be relentlessly active or live according to social expectations all the time. That life can be easier and lighter:

"What I will miss the most when I leave Argentina is this 'art de vivre', the lightness of life, the social and spontaneous aspect of everything, the everyday pleasures." (man, France, 1 year)

"Here people take the time to live: 'I'll stop by when I can…'. It used to irritate me but now it doesn't so much any more." (woman, France, 1 year)

"Life is simpler here – for example, what people expect of you. You're allowed to live in a relaxed way and enjoy things. In Holland we are always worried about things we have to do. Here I don't feel guilty when I am having a nice, pleasant time in my country house. In Holland, you always have to be doing lots of things." (man, Holland, 2 years)

"They always have work and a passion on the side: 'I work in a bookstore, but at night I do graphic design because it's my passion'. Argentines don't complain about their job, it's just work for them. They balance their life like that. Argentines take life in a much lighter way. People live to live." (woman, France, 2 months)

"They're more relaxed. In Spain, if you arrive late at work 3 times they send you home." (man, Spain, 15 months)

Francesco from Italy explains

Italians could learn a lot from Argentines about flexibility. Italy is now in crisis but in Argentina, where the crisis never stops, people still manage to disconnect from their political and economic problems and live in the present. Italians, on the other side, are completely depressed. Everything is not about politics and money. Argentines are able to stay on top of the bad mood generated by everyday problems. History taught them that happiness and humor cannot depend on these things.

Last but not least, Brazilians who have been living amongst Argentines (while being their eternal border rivals) discover that "happiness is not only a Brazilian trait".

"They know how to enjoy life more, I love that. They don't work as much, they take things more lightly than Brazilians (at least those from Sao Paulo). I love the fact that they go to public squares to exercise, have tea, have picnics, and hang around. People don't usually do that in Brazil." (woman, Brazil, 15 months)

"Here we learned that with little you can do much. People are not so worried about the crisis because they don't need as much to live." (man, Brazil, 7 months)

I believe this could be a niche for Argentines: they could offer a package of classes on 'how to balance the different aspects of life' and another on 'the fundamentals of Buen Vivir'. Foreigners, please note: if you buy both, you get a special discount!

7 : When in Argentina... take things with calm and patience

In previous small theories, I made the point that Argentines were very friendly; I also stated they were loyal and everyday superheroes... Now, like all true heroes, Argentine people also have their Achilles' heel.

I bet the first thing that comes to mind as their Achille's heel is the stereotype of the proud and arrogant Argentine. Well, that's not it. Arrogance is a trait that appears throughout my interviewees' answers, but only in a folkloric manner: yes, Argentines know everything, talk about anything with enthusiasm, are sweet talkers, never make mistakes, doesn't admit criticism (even of the constructive kind), and are never guilty... but that doesn't disturb foreigners too much.

The area in which the culture shock with Argentines is perceived to be the most negative is the one that has to do with their failure to honor commitments. Examples are overly abundant in my study, ranging from lack of punctuality to broken promises. However, this inability to meet obligations is even more disturbing when it occurs in the work sphere. For many of the interviewees it reflects a generalized disorganization, which never ceases to surprise them.

According to a Taiwanese interviewee: "You need to get used to it, or else your blood will constantly be boiling".

During my (relatively) short time living in this country, I have already learned never to be on time for a party, because the host might still be in pajamas, and that it's better to bring a book everywhere you go, just in case (thanks to all the waiting, I've become a very cultured person here in Buenos Aires!), or to have a backup plan. But I continue to have a harder time with business matters: even though I try to choose suppliers who deliver on schedule, I still get stressed out, I continue to fall into the trap of false expectations and still don't completely understand how things truly work. It feels like watching a domino line: since many people in a row don't deliver on what they promised, the only thing you can do is witness how the entire construction topples.

"They're not punctual at all. It's a nightmare having to wait for people to come to your house to repair things." (woman, Hungary, 3 months)

"[One of the things I will miss the least when I leave is] the lack of respect for people's time." (woman, United States, 2 years)

"[Something typically Argentine is] to say 'tomorrow' when it doesn't mean 'tomorrow'... (tomorrow, yes but, what year? what century?). Sometimes we call Argentina 'Mañanía'" (man, Russia, 11 years)

"In business, in politics, in private life, you can never really look forward to something with enthusiasm: there's always a complication, you can't rely on anything. I am still surprised by this after 10 years." (man, Holland, 15 years)

"People are less committed, unreliable. There is no maliciousness in that, they're just too laid-back. People here are not as ambitious as people from other countries." (woman, United Kingdom, 3 years)

"Sometimes they promise things and don't do them, just by fear of saying 'no'" (woman, Spain, 2 years)

"What bothers me the most is that, when they have to give a negative answer or are unable to do something, they don't say anything. They won't give a negative answer. They don't want to hurt the other person's feelings but it hurts more when they don't say anything. Then you find yourself left high and dry, alone on a Saturday night when all the other people already have plans." (woman, Holland, 4 years)

"There are differences in the perception of truth and lying… What I perceive as a lie is a means of expression or of socializing for them..." (woman, United States, 2 years)

Jennifer from Germany blogs

"The 10 things I will miss and not miss about living in Argentina" is a post in Jennifer Madison's blog, a German who lived in Argentine for three years. She writes: "Argentineans prefer confirming they will show up after receiving an invitation and canceling later, than canceling right away even though they already know they won't show up.

This has angered me quite a lot of times and it is something I definitely cannot get used to. I really need people around me that I can rely on and unfortunately, I was disappointed a lot in Argentina. Because quite a lot of times I invited my friends over to have dinner with us and many times, they just canceled on the spot. And this is not pleasant if you prepared a nice barbecue and bought the food and got really excited and then they send a cancellation by text message."

The failure to honor commitments gives an overall impression of lack of professionalism, which – in the opinion of the foreigners in this study – holds Argentines back in their local and international development. (In another of my small theories I praise the Argentine recipe for happiness, their balance between work and enjoyment... It's just that sometimes the balance is too much tilted towards the latter...)

Part of my job is to develop research methods and one day, an Argentine colleague told me that the digital applications we used in our company were made in the US or England. He thought, and I believe him, that they could be made in Argentina at a lesser cost but it's too risky, there is always the fear of people not delivering on time. By the way, I also find day-to-day communications unprofessional: emails have mistakes or include correspondence between other people that you don't want to or were not intended to see, invitations are sent the day before the event… It's as if the most important thing is to send something, anything, rather than the recipient.

"Argentines don't understand the concept of deadlines. They promise you things and I am chasing them for a week. I need to meet a deadline in London, and they end up thinking I am slack" (woman, United Kingdom, 3 years)

"Slow to answer, bad at communication." (woman, United States, 4 months)

"They don't do things on the spot, they don't answer emails. In Italy you have to answer on the spot." (man, Italy, 3 years)

"They are unambitious at work, not very competitive and inefficient… [When I leave] I won't miss the absence of a well-functioning business system." (man, Holland, 5 years)

"The Argentine is lazy and doesn't deliver… Since I am a hard worker, this gives me more opportunities." (man, Italy, 15 months)

71

"Mexicans are more willing to work than Argentines: if they have work they tend to it. The Argentine worker arrives at 9:30 and leaves quickly at 5pm. They lack the motivation of knowing that work is important." (woman, Mexico, 4 years)

"They don't have a very pronounced sense of responsibility. "(man, China, 2 years)

"Difficulties with the provision of services. The technician says he will come and then doesn't. Waiting two months to set up the Internet: it's worse than Brazil." (man, Brazil, 2 years)

"The younger people are not responsible at all at work: they leave, don't show up, come to work sometimes, they don't care. I had to increase the average age of workers in my firm." (man, Spain, 2 years)

"Sometimes at work they tell you pretty obvious things like 'you'll need to be there between 8 and 12'. To me that is normal, but it shows that there are people who don't do it." (woman, Italy, 3 years)

"Poor client service. Employees talk to each other while helping you, or instead of doing so." (man, Brazil, 2 years)

"The client is never right, the one who's right is the owner of the business." (woman, Mexico, 4 years)

"They don't work in a diligent manner: they leave loose cables, broken edges... And in the end it looks unfinished, basic details are missing." (man, Russia, 11 years)

"They're opportunistic, they don't try to build long-lasting business relations. Immediate gains are more important to them than a 10-year plan." (woman, Japan, 14 years)

After several experiences, I realized that Argentines actually do deliver on what they promised, but without keeping the client informed or communicating the process to them. It has happened to me that, after waiting for a long time without any form of news or update and starting to think that I am probably never going to get what I asked for, all of a sudden the supplier calls to tell me my order is ready and I have to pay right away.

Maria from Brazil recalls

I used to go to a sports club to exercise and play tennis. At one point I had two classes to make up and on a bright, sunny day, under the intense blue sky that you can only find in Argentina, I ran into my coach. He was sitting on the terrace, enjoying the morning sun. Since he didn't seem busy, I suggested that we could recover my classes at that moment. He told me he was unavailable. "But you don't have any students right now" I said, somewhere between surprised and offended. "No, I can't", he replied, "because this is the time I set aside to drink mate".

The perceived lack of organization definitely does not help to create a climate of trust. There probably is some kind of order (as Shakespeare said, "Though this be madness, yet there is method in it"), but this order is difficult to understand for us foreigners.

"It's always like a nice chaos: Argentines don't do simple things, like make a list, for instance. They think things will fall into place by themselves." (woman, Holland, 5 years)

"[My first impressions of Argentines was] generalized disorganization". (woman, France, 2 years)

"They wait in lines for hours. If they were a bit more organized, they wouldn't need that many lines." (woman, China, 4 months)

"[What I will miss the least when I leave] is the disorder." (man, Russia, 11 years)

Wherever you go, you will always find things that make you feel uncomfortable. Cultural shock tends to be less violent however when one is aware of the other's habits and expectations. In the US, for instance, it is considered good service to wait on customers quickly in restaurants: remove the plates as soon as they finish eating and bring the bill as early as possible. The result is that foreigners often feel pushed out. Yet, contrary to what one could think, the motive behind this is quite considerate: it is to ensure that the client doesn't waste time. Quite the opposite of "taking things with calm and patience", isn't it?

M. from Holland recalls

Argentines don't know how to plan. That's why they don't succeed collectively in a lot of things. I used to sail regattas with six people. We would never win. Each time one of the members of the group had a problem, all the others abandoned their position to go help that person. It was very friendly, but not so efficient… So I started to put some order. We ended up winning… but they called me Hitler!

8 : Argentines lack team spirit

Many interviewees agree that Argentines sometimes have little respect for the basic norms of social coexistence. This behavior that can be summarized in three words: lack of civility.

Here's an example: in the worldwide distribution of resources, Argentina was endowed with an incredible nature. Buenos Aires is a beautiful city, with dreamlike weather that both natives and foreigners deeply miss when they have to leave.

"When I leave Argentina, I'll miss the landscapes, and traveling miles and miles without seeing a single building." (man, France, 15 years)

"The vegetation, the magnificent trees." (man, Holland, 9 months)

"Buenos Aires is a beautiful city, I love the history, the houses, the cobble stone streets, statues, parks...trees and flowers, all year round there is always something blooming, blue skies." (woman, United States, 2 years)

"Parks are so beautiful, I love the trees, so pretty." (woman, Aruba, 9 months)

"The city's layout with its huge parks." (woman, Hungary, 3 months)

"The city, the streets with trees, the vegetation, the colors, the birds... To have all of this inside a city." (man, Brazil, 2 years)

"I'll miss the blue sky, it's very difficult to see it in China." (man, China, 2 years)

And yet, Argentines don't necessarily respect their environment:

"My neighbor's dog's poo, her kids throwing candy wrappings in my garden: that's not something you do." (woman, France, 1 year)

"I won't miss the garbage in the street." (woman, Holland, 4 years)

"There's no environmental awareness, no recycling, they are way behind compared to other countries in that regard. They could respect nature a little more and teach their children about the environmental consequences of their actions." (woman, Spain, 2 years)

"One of the things I like least about Argentina is the trash issue, there is a low level of consciousness and conscientiousness regarding public space hygiene. Not throwing your alfajor[15] wrapper on the ground." (man, United States, 6 years)

---

[15] Alfajor is a traditional Argentine sweet.

"Dog poo. Buildings ruined by graffiti." (woman, Great Britain, 9 months)

"What I will miss the least is the filthiness. Drivers throwing things out the window. People need to be made aware that only they can make a change: by keeping the place clean, helping others…" (woman, Aruba, 9 months)

Some foreigners are also astonished by the waste of natural resources. A Taiwanese interviewee told me that when Chinese people arrive here they tend to be amazed by the abundant use of water and gas: having almost free water and using it to clean the sidewalk seems unbelievable!

"The waste of water!" (woman, India, 2 years)

"Doormen wash the sidewalk with LITERS of water every morning. You have to consider the entire system, other people's needs. In this case, saving water and helping out a little." (man, Colombia, 4 years)

This peculiarity is something that even Argentines acknowledge. According to Marco Denevi[16]: The common Argentine has the mentality of a hotel guest, the hotel is the country and they are a tourist who doesn't interact with the others. If the hotel managers do a poor job, if they steal and make inaccurate accounting records then that's the owner's problem, not that of the guests, whose own future house, still under

---

[16] Argentine writer (1922-1988), unofficial translation of quote by Kist

construction, is waiting for them someplace else (...)
Maybe one day we Argentines will convince ourselves
that this transit hotel is our only home, and that there's
no other Argentina – visible or invisible – waiting for us in
another place.

In addition to the environmental aspect, many
interviewees see a lack of civility in the failure to respect
others and in the different forms of everyday abuse. The
best example of this is perhaps what Argentines call
"*viveza criolla*[17]", where the habit of taking advantage
of the other reaches its maximum expression.

---

[17] *Viveza criolla (criollo cleverness)* is a philosophy existing in Latin
American societies which tends to legitimate a certain selfishness and
the disrespect of moral codes in situations when one's interest is at
stake. Corruption is an example of this. In the eyes of its advocates,
viveza criolla is the only way of surviving and/or progressing in an
extremely individualistic society.

Viveza criolla works very well with foreigners but it is also used among themselves. What I find particularly surprising is the strong contrast between the "warm" and "loyal" behavior towards friends and relatives (as described in theories 2 and 5) and this unpleasant conduct in the anonymity of public space. Another Argentine paradox!

"They don't think of the other, but always seek their own benefit. Argentines need to see themselves as part of the system because they are very egocentric." (man, Colombia, 4 years)

"Some take advantage of the fact that I am a foreigner and charge me more." (woman, Italy, 3 years)

"They don't let other people talk – instead they speak over you in a louder tone, that's how they take the floor." (woman, Venezuela, 20 months)

"Taking others as hostages to make political demands… The right to strike is a good thing but disturbing others in the maximum way in order to be heard is annoying… Unions could have a more cooperative approach." (man, France, 1 year)

"They don't care about others. When I am taking a short nap after lunch in my office [a very common thing to do in China], they could take me into consideration, but they keep on making noise. Many people in my company come from China: we have to respect Argentines but they too should respect us also." (man, China, 2 years)

"[One of Argentines' weaknesses is] viveza criolla. They think they are so clever. Someone comes to repair and he does a poor job and charges you too much and thinks he's smart." (man, United States, 6 years)

"They are dishonest, don't inspire trust. We Chileans are afraid they will cheat us: they don't trust themselves or other people." (woman, Chile, 6 years)

"In business, stay away from them! There are no ethical codes. The gentlemen's agreement doesn't exist, not with a handshake and not even when it is written." (man, Italy, 7 years)

"They are street smart but I don't know if I admire it. They are always looking to tilt the playing field to get more. Our landlord makes us pay in the US so she doesn't pay taxes." (woman, United States, 17 months)

"Here people boast about not paying taxes! They're proud of it. If the police arrest you, 'justice is a failure', if you don't pay taxes it's because taxes are excessive or go to politician's pockets. This opens a whole spectrum of "anything goes" due to lack of trust in the system and the absence of the idea of a common good." (woman, Spain, 3 years)

That *viveza criolla* is part of national identity is something few people would deny. It's like mate or dulce de leche. And they enjoy it: while foreigners see *viveza criolla* as a flaw, true Argentines cannot avoid smiling when they are confronted with the topic.

However, many interviewees observe that this behavior ends up causing a real trust issue, with serious repercussions in many areas: economics, politics, social life and even happiness.[18]

S. from Aruba recalls

One day I went to Carrefour to do my weekly shopping. Since I had just come out of the gym, I carried a bottle of water and a cereal bar with me. I didn't manage to find a trashcan in the supermarket, so when I arrived at the checkout both the bottle and the cereal bar wrapping were in my shopping cart.

When the cashier saw them, she called security. They told me there was no way I could prove I had bought them somewhere else – and not stolen them from the shelves – so I had to pay for them. I replied that in Carrefour you could only buy cereal bars in six-packs. And they accused me of opening one.

Why would I do something like that? I got so angry I left my full shopping cart and left. This lack of common sense is unbelievable: I was about to make a major purchase and they lost it... because of a cereal bar!

---

[18] Trust and freedom have positive effects on happiness (in "the pursuit of happiness", Carol Graham)

"They always think someone is cheating them, they can't trust anyone. An example: I offer someone to work 12 hours for me, telling him I will pay him the extra hours, feed him, etc., and they say we are exploiting them; they take on the role of victims. There's no trust." (man, Colombia, 4 years)

In some interviews, the lack of civility perceived in Argentina comes across though another of the country's weaknesses: discrimination.

"There's racism towards neighboring countries." (woman, France, 7 years)

"There's discrimination - for instance, against homosexuals. Argentines have a hard time making space for the opinion of others." (woman, Holland, 5 years)

"They form superficial judgments about foreigners. If you are Spanish or Italian, they immediately like you because of their roots. If you are from Chile or Great Britain they hate you because of historic incidents from years back. If you are a foreigner from South America they despise you." (woman, Spain, 2 years)

"Those with higher socioeconomic status enjoy being in their position and belittling others." (woman, Brazil, 2 years)

"People in the poor areas: "los negros"[19], as they call them here…" (woman, Italy, 3 years)

"While revering people from Europe and the United States, they sometimes have a discriminative attitude towards other South American countries and people from Asia." (woman, Great Britain, 3 years)

"Argentines treat Brazilians differently than they do people from other countries. One of the parents at my daughter's school is a Brazilian married to a Bolivian. They used to live in the United States: when they say they come from the US they are treated in a certain way; when she says she is Brazilian, then it's different." (woman, Brazil, 15 months)

"They treat me nicely when they learn I'm from Mexico. They like Mexico, but not Brazil!" (woman, Mexico, 2 years)

"Argentines like to work with Paraguayans. They discriminate Bolivians and Chileans a lot." (man, Paraguay, 2 years)

"There's a lot of discrimination. When I first arrived here they called me "chinita"[20], and never called me by my real name." (woman, Korea, 14 years)

---

[19] *Negro* means black in Spanish but is often used in a pejorative way to talk about people with darker skin, of African descent or not.

[20] *Chinita* is the diminutive for "china" (= Chinese).

I myself have witnessed situations which I found discriminatory. When I arrived in this country, I took Spanish classes at a university in Buenos Aires. The classes were intended for foreign students and most of them were exchange students, living in Argentine homes. One of the students was African American, and the family that hosted her called her "Negrita"[21]. She was so offended that she complained to the program director but they just explained that in Argentina, it was an expression of affection.

In *"Culture Shock Argentina (a survival guide to customs and etiquette)"*, Fiona Adams explains: "All this [nicknames etc...] may seem shockingly racist, 'sizeist', 'ageist' and 'looksist' but no insult is meant at all...it's actually meant affectionately." To me, it is still discrimination, even if it is meant to be kind.

Using the phrase in its best (but also its worst) acceptance, one American interviewee accurately summed things up: "Argentina is the exact opposite of politically correct".

---

[21] *Negrita* is the diminutive for "negra" (= black).

9 : Argentines are somewhat adolescent

I remember reading a study a few years ago that defined the US as a teenage country. Not because it is a relatively young nation, but because its people act in ways that are characteristic of teenagers. I don't know how reliable the study was overall, but this statement came to my mind when I moved to Argentina.

Like teenagers, Argentines are constantly in search of their identity and sometimes tend to exaggerate and act impulsively, don't you agree? Whoever has experienced a teenager at home knows that everything is always their parents' fault, that they are responsible for -completely and permanently- ruining the youngster's life.

Is it because Argentines stay in their parents' house for so many years that they never finish growing up?

"I like that family is important here – we ship our kids off at 16, 17, 18 years old and they don't come back. Argentines stay with their family until older and come home for family meals." (woman, United States, 2 years)

"In Colombia at 28 it's normal to go live on your own and to have finished your studies. Here at 28 they live with their parents and start a third degree because they didn't finish the previous ones. It's as if they were 18." (man, Colombia, 4 years)

In this quest for identity, the classic Argentine oscillation between feeling very European at times and very Latino at others clearly appears. They are great cosmopolitans, yes, but from their little back yard. "The first thing that strikes visitors to Argentina is whether the Argentines are Latin Americans or Europeans who through a strange twist of fate have been uprooted and thrown into the middle of South America...Culturally and emotionally, Argentina remains firmly attached to Europe and its eyes are continually straining across the Atlantic for inspiration and approval." (Fiona Adams in "Culture Shock Argentina")

"They always refer to themselves as European rather than Argentine. I am English but have Scottish and Swiss blood too, but I never refer to myself as anything other than English." (woman, Great Britain, 3 years)

"They identify with Europeans. It would disturb them not to be Europeans. I don't really understand the relevance of "my great grandfather was Italian so I'm a bit Italian", especially if you take into account that those Italians fled their country!" (woman, France, 6 months)

This teenage-like fervor put into denigrating one's own family – or, in this case, the culture you have always lived in –, this rebellion against their land is typically Argentine. Except when it comes to defending the colors of the "Albiceleste" team, Argentines are wolves to other Argentines, they are their worst critics, and their most passionate detractors.

"They're not very proud of their country – it's the first time I see people not proud of their country." (woman, Aruba, 9 months)

"Incredibly self-deprecating, self-critical … More so than in other countries, 'we are a bunch of fools', 'este país')" (man, United States, 6 years)

"One of the problems Argentines have is their fascination with Europe and the US. But there is a lot of excellence here. Designs are very good, but they still look to other countries and try to imitate them. In Italy we value authentic culture, its typical elements." (man, Italy, 3 years)

"Argentines are full of paradox. They complain a lot but they love their country and would never leave." (woman, France, 2 years)

In fact, all these feelings appear to coexist and end up producing an identity that is eclectic but also unique and fascinating.

As to Argentine impulsiveness and their tendency to exaggerate, let me share a couple of keys to demystify them.

THEY ARE DRAMA QUEENS.

And their anthem is tango: melancholic and sad, with no happy ending. (Is it possible to be more explicit than Catulo Castillo in his song *El desencuentro* that goes: "That's why in your total failure to live, you'll even miss your final shot"?). Argentines are fond of emphatic words and permanently use *non plus ultra* expressions: "terrific", "superb", "phenomenal", "spectacular", "I'm dying", "you killed me", "I can't believe it!", "I adore it", "how divine!"

"They switch very quickly [in a conversation] from 'idols' to 'less than nothings': you are either the best or the worst". (man, France, 15 years)

"Drama is particularly Argentine. 'Polar winter' when it's 60º F outside! They are funny. […] They are very dramatic about everything. This explains why they always say they are worse than they are." (woman, Brazil, 2 years)

The drama is said to filter into romantic life as well, namely through jealous or hysteric behaviors.

Of course, I wouldn't know, since I am definitely not in the dating scene, but various interviewees have come across this very Argentine characteristic in their intimate relationships.

"In Europe I have a lot of male friends who are like my sister to me, but that is not possible here, there is this jealousy thing. I miss having normal friendships with male friends, with no hidden agenda." (woman, France, 2 months)

"At work I sometimes have lunch with female colleagues, and my male colleagues ask me if my girlfriend knows about this. Having women friends is not normal here." (man, Holland, 2 years)

"Women are a bit neurotic, they are always talking about other women." (man, Holland, 5 months)

"Argentines are hysterical when it comes to romantic relationships. So much jealousy! Women have manners and tricks which most of the time I don't understand." (woman, Holland, 4 years)

"When you date someone, there's a lot of "histeriqueo²²", beating around the bush and playing with one another's feelings: I like you but I won't say it, I say the opposite of what I mean and you just have to understand. Relationships are so complicated, I don't know how they reproduce." (man, Colombia, 4 years)

"They are jealous inside their couple, they get mad at each other, they have macho attitudes" (man, Italy, 3 years)

"There is a lot of hysteria in romantic relationships. It's a question of ego, there's a big lack of trust." (man, Spain, 4 years)

---

²² *Histeriqueo* is inherent to the Argentine style of seduction. It originates from the word "histérica" (designating a woman who will refuse to sleep with a man) and is used to describe attitudes of people (male or female) who, when flirting with someone, will beat around the bush and be inconsistent, not clearly expressing their intentions, disappearing and reappearing, sending contradictory messages, etc. The person guilty of this is then called "histérico" or "histérica".

DRAMA QUEENS ARE EGOCENTRIC.

"They believe Argentina is a completely distinct place, that it doesn't belong to the rest of the world. They think what happens to them only happens to them." (woman, Spain, 13 years)

"They are egocentric, not because they think they are the best but because they are convinced at an individual level that the world turns around them." (man, Colombia, 4 years)

"The culture of me, myself and I." (woman, Chile, 6 years)

ALL EGOCENTRICS WANT TO LOOK GOOD.

As we saw in a previous theory, Argentines are basically attractive and physical appearance is something that people value, but sometimes they go too far. It is widely known that Argentine women suffer in order to be thin (and their gym efforts seem more geared towards this goal than towards that of general well-being). But what about surgeries? If these women are already attractive, is it really necessary to go through an intervention that will make them look all alike?

"Looks are important here and women are insecure about their appearance, you can tell from their expression." (man, Holland, 5 months)

"They are obsessed with what foreigners think about Argentines. They are obsessed with their looks, with vanity." (woman, United Kingdom, 3 years)

"Women don't eat, it's impressive how they live just worried about their physical beauty... In Brazil they do surgeries, here there's a culture of not eating." (woman, Brazil, 15 months)

"They are obsessed with their body, but always through the lens of the other's perspective. They want to be pretty but always identical to each other: same hair, same clothes, same thinness." (woman, Brazil, 4 years)

AND ALL TEENAGERS ARGUE WITH THEIR PARENTS AND BLAME THEM FOR EVERYTHING.

"Argentines complain more than they act, they waste their opportunities." (man, Spain, 1 year)

"They can never accept that they were wrong, apologizing is impossible here, everyone gets offended." (woman, Brazil, 4 years)

"It's never their fault, they always give explanations: it's the government, it's the instability... It's a pity." (woman, France, 7 years)

"[In business] everything always has to be negotiated. Direct orders don't work." (man, Spain, 2 years)

"Communicating with employees is a nightmare: whenever they receive orders they question their meaning, argue, and don't make any effort to understand... In China one would first try to understand what the company's interest is." (man, China, 2 years)

"They get offended easily, are incapable of introspection because it's never their fault. They have a hard time making space for the opinion of others." (woman, Holland, 5 years)

"Politics are childish, everything is based on what happens in Argentina. They don't have any realistic images of what happens in the rest of the world." (man, Holland, 2 years)

"Politicians here speak like a father to his child, like Berlusconi used to do. Twenty years ago, Italian politicians could still get away with this behavior. Now we are more aware." (man, Italy, 3 years)

"They see the other as an enemy, don't know how to collaborate… In politics, for instance, getting 51% of the vote means 49% of the population didn't vote for you. You have to take this into account, you can't just force your will onto people without any nuance. Democracy isn't the will of the majority but the will of the people. It's the same with all the conspiracy theories, when Argentines think the rest of the people (sometimes entire countries) are against them." (man, Holland, 15 years)

"They have to stop being victims and start trusting themselves, be positive and solve the problem." (woman, Japan, 14 years)

It always surprises me that Argentines view their government as a group of extraterrestrials controlling the country, without anybody knowing where they came from or how to stop them. When applied to Argentina,

95

the notion that government should be "by the people, for the people" [23] changes to "by the government, for the people who comply (or not)".

Collective awareness of each person's role as a citizen and actor of the system always seems to be lacking, and so does the capacity for dialogue. Therefore, Argentines feel entitled to clamor, once and again, as true teenagers would...

YOU (THE COUNTRY, **THEIR** COUNTRY) RUINED MY LIFE!

---

[23] *Government* of the *people, by the people, for the people,* Abraham Lincoln in Gettysburg address (1863)

10 : Argentines can be proud of their country

One thing is the image you have of yourself, another thing is the way others perceive you. Jokes about the Argentine ego abound, and my personal favorite is the one that goes: "How does an Argentine commit suicide? By jumping off their own ego!". I find it nicely depicts the Argentine paradox between arrogance and melancholy. (Or between inferiority and superiority, but I am no psychologist; and even if I were, Argentina doesn't need one more, as it is already famous for having the highest number of psychologists per capita in the world...).

Hereunder are the achievements of Argentines as a society which were put forward by the foreigners interviewed for this book. Clearly, there are many reasons... not to jump!

Asado

"I like their parrillas (grills) or asados because they are centered around a social atmosphere, it's not 'wam bang', in-out, let's throw some burgers on the grill." (man, United States, 6 months)

"Argentine grills are advanced! US people love them! Compared to our little Weber grills..." (man, United States, 6 years)

"The best thing ever invented is the asado!" (man, Taiwan, 15+ years)

"In this country, I became addicted to 'asado de tira' (short ribs)." (woman, Mexico, 4 years)

Asado seen from the outside

When I arrived in Argentina and began looking for a house to rent, the woman from the real estate agency constantly referred to the quincho (or barbecue area) as if it were the most important part of the house. I didn't even know what a quincho was because I had never seen one or suffered from its absence in my previous homes. Each country has its particularities: in France, it's very important to have separate toilets; in the US, what matters is the brand of the household appliances and the type of wood on the floor... In any case, now that I have a quincho I certainly don't want to lose it!

Mate

"They are obsessed with their socializing tradition with mate!" (woman, United Kingdom, 3 years)

"In Holland we no longer know how to take time to do things like sit down to have mate, share with others. In Argentina there is more of a group culture." (woman, Holland, 4 years)

The experience of *mate* seen from the outside

"Never say no to a mate. Avoid making faces after you've swallowed it, even though the bitterness of this potion may well surprise the European palate", says the French guidebook "Guides Etat du Monde – Argentine" (Ludovic Lamant).

Clearly, one of my Colombian interviewees didn't read this guidebook: "One day I declined a mate and the people around me got offended, it's an obsession." (man, Colombia, 4 years)

Although it is a strange and difficult habit for foreigners (my husband had to explain the codes to me), it's like the DNI : you know you were born and raised in Argentina when the simple thought that drinking mate is equivalent to passing germs between friends has never crossed your mind.

Wine

"China and Argentina have a good relationship today and there is a lot of business, we import beef, red wine and mate – they are getting more popular (before the wine was from France and Chile)." (man, China, 2 years)

"Wine, champagne, I will miss them so much!" (woman, Mexico, 4 years)

"I'll miss the wine, it is so expensive in Korea." (woman, Korea, 14 years)

Wine and the power of innovation

I read Malbec is an example of a great Argentine accomplishment. Before, the country used to produce a low-quality Malbec using a harvesting protocol directly from France, where the variety originally grew. In the years 2000, a new protocol was created thanks to research by oenologists. It was adapted to Argentina through innovation in the growing method and in the watering pattern.

As a result, a superior Malbec was produced which, thanks to a successful marketing strategy, is now internationally renowned.

Tango

"Foreigners are fascinated by tango." (man, Taiwan, 20+ years)

"Music, tango, the fact that it is preserved – I admire that." (woman, Aruba, 9 months)

"I admire tango, their passion for art and dance." (man, United States, 6 months)

Soccer

"They manage to have good players, Maradona, Messi. They keep finding and training good players. I'm a soccer fan, soccer matches are more fun here than in Brazil. They sing all the time and cheer, more than in Brazil (even though according to our reputation we should be the ones singing!). It's a very emotional experience." (woman, Brazil, 2 years)

"Argentines could teach the Chinese how to play soccer! China has a hard time entering the World Cup, we can't find a sufficient number of good players, despite our population being so large!" (man, China, 2 years)

"I love their obsession with soccer. Everyone loves soccer. So much passion." (woman, United Kingdom, 2 months)

"They beat Holland in the World Cup!" (woman, Holland, 4 years)

"Soccer is a passion they develop when they are kids and that they experience through Messi. It's a quality because it unites them, gives them an identity and makes them proud. Messi is even on milk and bread packages." (woman, Venezuela, 20 months)

The variety of cultural and artistic activities

"I love the quantity of artists exhibiting their work. Theatres are easily accessible, anyone can go. It's a good thing!" (woman, France, 7 years)

"They don't realize what they have in Bellas Artes, and MALBA! Constantini is one of the biggest collectors in the world. The art scene is amazing. Art courses here are much more developed than the ones we have in Brazil. People from all over Latin America come here to take courses, including teachers." (woman, Brazil, 2 years)

"The Argentine cinema industry has a worldwide reputation." (woman, France, 6 months)

"Literature, Argentine authors, art in general. They are very creative." (woman, Spain, 2 years)

"I admire their creativity. There is a lot of street art, these great amazing graffiti pieces, real works of art." (woman, United Kingdom, 3 years)

"Everything surrounding cultural life is perfect: the cultural offer, the organization." (man, Colombia, 4 years)

"Culture is very much encouraged, both on an official level and in the private sphere." (man, Italy, 3 years)

"The culture, the vast number of high-quality courses. There's a huge offer, and it's available to everyone." (woman, Chile, 6 years)

Argentina's museums seen from the outside

I love the texts that accompany the exhibitions and works of art in museums here (in MALBA, for instance, or in the Van Gogh digital exhibition at Usina del Arte). They are short, intelligent and go straight to the point. Congratulations!

Argentines in the World

"I admire the fact that they always stand out. In every sport as well as in other fields, you always see an Argentine person triumphing. The best tennis player, the best formula one driver, the best ballet dancer, now the Pope... An Argentine man penetrated the most closed place in the world." (woman, Uruguay, 6 years)

"Maradona did a lot of good things in Italy. Here no one likes him but in Italy he gave financial support to many people. He helped children with heart problems." (woman, Italy, 6 years)

"Messi and his humility. Argentines are extravagant but Messi isn't, that's why he's such a good ambassador for Argentina." (man, United States, 6 years)

Pope Francis, who "shows Argentina in a good light".

Eva Peron, "fascinating, magical and she died young".

Che Guevara, who "remains a symbol for many people in the world".

Burman, Darín, who "represent Argentina across the world".

Máxima, "the Queen of Holland".

Borges, "they are proud of him".

Biro, "he invented the ballpoint pen or "birome" in Spanish" (he was actually Hungarian but the invention is attributed to Argentina).

Fangio, "an internationally-known athlete".

Their scientific standing

"Agriculture is very advanced in Argentina" (woman, Holland, 5 years) – *It is said they are leaders in the third agricultural revolution.*

"They have great scientists who are recognized across the world." (man, France, 15 years)

"They have several Nobel prizes, namely in chemistry. And there's the Leloir Institute[24]." (woman, Holland, 4 years)

"I visited several centers: they have some cutting-edge technology, and bright, educated, very talented scientists and engineers in the country. Although with import restrictions and other obstacles it's difficult for these professionals to do their jobs and be competitive." (man, United States, 6 months)

"There is an Argentine woman who holds a very high position at NASA. So does an Argentine judge in the international court." (woman, Holland, 5 years)

"They have an advanced level in scientific research. For instance, L'Oréal has a "L'Oreal-Unesco women in science award" which is granted to a woman each year. Argentine women won several times!" (woman, Venezuela, 20 months)

According to Wikipedia, Argentina was awarded the L'Oréal prize three times across the total of 18 sessions of the competition, thus putting Argentina in a salient place with respect to the size of its population. Argentines also won 5 Nobel Prizes (three out of which were obtained in hard sciences), a record for Latin America (www.nobelprize.org).

---

[24] Luis Federico Leloir (1906-87), a biochemist, was the first South American to receive a Nobel Prize in chemistry, and the third to win a Nobel Prize.

The bus network

"The bus system is magical (once you understand it) and safe." (woman, France, 6 months)

"The transportation: I do everything by bus. You can go home by bus at any time of the night. It's very well organized and efficient, given the price you pay. And the SUBE transportation card is a major improvement." (woman, Holland, 4 years)

"Transportation by bus works really well. There are about 1000 bus lines that work all night long, it's a luxury!" (woman, Spain, 2 years)

"Not the trains, not the subways but the bus system. I am impressed by it. Compared to US buses, they are not as pretty and clean but there are hundreds of bus lines. That little piece of the transportation system works really well." (man, United States, 6 years)

"The public transportation system works particularly well: it's efficient, reliable and accessible." (woman, Brazil, 4 months)

"Travelling in Argentina is easy: I've only had good experiences." (woman, France, 1 year)

Proximity services

"Everything is delivered to your home: groceries, toys, pet food, mineral water, chlorine, car wash… You don't get that in Europe. Europeans would be embarrassed to be helped so directly." (woman, Spain, 2 years)

"They deliver ice cream to your home in the middle of the night! The drug store brought me two blisters of Ibuprofen!" (woman, France, 7 years)

"You can get anything delivered to your door – I recently had two bottles of Tequila delivered." (man, United States, 8 years)

"The magic of the kiosco[25]." (woman, France, 1 year)

"The small verduleria stands (=greengrocers) everywhere, having fresh produce so close to you (versus the food deserts in the US) is convenient – People coming from outside really notice and appreciate it." (man, United States, 6 years)

"The services are really good quality. Professionals make house calls (vets, doctors). It shocked me in a good way." (man, United States, 6 months)

"The local butcher knows your name, they recognize you in the pasta store – the warmth comes out in day to day interactions." (woman, United States, 2 year)

_____

[25] In Argentina, kiosks (*kioscos*) are very common. They not only sell newspapers and magazines but all sorts of other products: sweets, cigarettes, beverages, mate, hot sandwiches, etc.

And (some) public services

"Public university. Argentines are very prepared, more than Italians." (man, Italy, 2 years)

"The education: lots of people study and continue to study their entire life. And on top of that, it's free." (man, Italy, 3 years)

Public university seen from the outside

"Here, anyone who wishes to do so can study. As a Dutch person, I can study here for free and I am SO thankful for it that I always do things to give back, for instance giving blood. I am also impressed by the educational offer: they have three different "shifts" at university for each course, to make it easier for those who are working." (woman, Holland, 4 years)

"The education system, both private and public. In the private sector, the possibility of bilingual education: access to bilingual schools is relatively cheap. In Brazil I couldn't afford it, here I can. I know someone who has kids in the public sector and they offer extended schedules for parents who work, various sports..." (woman, Brazil, 1 year)

"The universal health care system. In Mexico they have it too, but I think hospitals are worse." (woman, Mexico, 2 years)

"In Buenos Aires province the public health service is good. I went to an ophthalmology hospital, waited a bit and they attended me without charges. In Holland, I would have had to wait longer to see a doctor. Here they gave me results of a blood analysis in 2 hours!" (man, Holland, 2 years)

"The garbage collection: they pick up the garbage regularly… In France you need to bring your branches and all your garden waste to a special place and you have to pay." (woman, France, 1 year)

The weather and outdoor facilities

"Buenos Aires is a beautiful city. There are parks, a lot of bike roads. It's very easy to do things outdoors, become member of a sports club." (woman, Brazil, 2 years)

"The weather is great. It took me 10 years to stop thinking that I had to go outside every time the sun was shining." (man, Holland, 15 years)[26]

"The weather… In Paraguay it's 45°C in the summer, you sweat just sitting down." (man, Paraguay, 2 years)

"They have the perfect spring: not cold, not hot, beautiful days, everything is green." (man, Colombia, 4 years)

---

[26] In Holland sunny days are so rare that when the sun does come out, everybody hurries outside to enjoy it. Sometimes they just put a chair on the sidewalk.

Finally, and because every Argentine person is unique and inimitable, here goes a list of other unique and inimitable Argentine achievements our foreign interviewees chose to highlight. Sit back, relax, sip a mate and enjoy.

- Their struggle for human rights
- Their struggle for political ideals
- Their solidarity
- Gay rights
- Labor legislation
- The possibility for immigrants to build a future
- The night life
- The music, Argentine rock
- The diversity: living with such a mix of people
- A kind of "positive anarchy": "there's this sense of freedom, an essential freedom in everyday life, a way of not placing themselves under constant rules that has a positive side to it."
- Their creativity in marketing
- Their parties and party services
- There is a day for everything (for children, for teachers, for employees...)
- Club life
- Caring for one's appearance and body
- Sports in general
- Dog walkers
- Flattering compliments in the street
- The "Pago Facil" outlet (= a place where you can pay all kinds of bills)

- Gauchito Gil[27] and Difunta Correa[28]
- The flour and the milk
- Empanadas[29]
- Chimichurri[30]
- Facturas[31]
- Dulce de leche[32]

And for me: the tapas criollas from La Salteña. I'm a very bad cook but I still haven't found the way to ruin them. They always turn out well!

---

[27] Gauchito Gil is a legendary figure in Argentina's popular history. The story goes that this hard-working *gaucho* entered the army to escape a feud with relatives but was captured and sentenced to death after deserting. Just before his execution, he told his hangman that his son was ill and asked him to pray for him in his name. The executioner found his ill son, and after praying for him in the name of Gauchito Gil the son survived, thus starting the cult around Gil's figure.

[28] Difunta Correa is also a mythical figure in Argentina. She is said to have secretly followed her husband after he was enrolled in one of the country's civil wars. While attempting to follow the troops in the San Juan desert, she died of thirst and exhaustion. The survival of her baby (who was with her) was interpreted as her first miracle.

[29] *Empanadas* are stuffed pastries containing meat, eggs, or other ingredients, and very popular in Latin America.

[30] *Chimichurri* is an uncooked sauce used to accompany grilled meat. It contains garlic, parsley, oil, vinegar and oregano.

[31] Argentine version of pastries/sweet rolls (similar to croissants etc...)

[32] One of Argentina's flagship products, *dulce de leche* is obtained by heating sweetened milk to create a thick substance that resembles caramel.

A happy ending

At the beginning of this book I observed that everybody thinks differently but, at the same time, everybody thinks they are right. As I reach the end of it, I believe it is thanks to our contacts with others that we manage to understand and define ourselves. So what did I learn about myself along the way? Mainly that I was definitely not crazy to move to this country. Living in Argentina has enriched my life and transformed me.

Every day I am amazed by the conversations I have with people I don't know. I enjoy their warmth and I talk more than I used to!

I am also amazed by Argentine people's capacity to find solutions to life. To their own lives, but also sometimes unsolicited ones for mine: "You should really do this this way… If you do it like this, it will be faster/cheaper…"

Not every day – but a lot more often than before – I wonder about the relative values of happiness and economic well-being. This eternal question (everyone knows money does not equal happiness, and everyone rejoices when *celebrities* are unhappy) took on an entirely new dimension for me in Argentina. I am not sure anymore whether I prefer to do something useful or take time to chat with someone I like …

There are also things I used to take for granted that

took on a new dimension: the value of good government, the respect for all citizens and their liberties. And the importance of trusting others and the system.

They say progress of mankind is the result of sparks of creativity which occur when different cultures or civilizations meet. Although it may not be progress for mankind, writing this book was an important step for me: I now know that the next time I review one of my mental *checklists*, I'll remember that Argentine man who explained that weekends are for having an *asado* with friends and looking at the sky.

Acknowledgements

I want to thank all the foreigners who trusted me and willingly accepted to take part in my study. They are: Emily, Jantine, Dirk, Maarten and Serge from The Netherlands; Catherine, Catherine, Julie, Sophie, Frederic and Nicolas from France; Alicia, Laura, Verónica, Adrián, Iñigo and Víctor from Spain; Mariana, Francesco, Giordano and Michele from Italy; Sarah and Sophie from Great Britain, Arthur from Russia and Sophia from Hungary; Alexis, Ana, Rika, Susan, Susie, Bryant, Gary, Raymond and Rick from the United States; Camila, Flavia, Juliana, Marcele, Michelle, Edvan, Ricardo (with Elena) and Wlamir from Brasil; Andrea from Uruguay; Claudia from Venezuela; Mónica from Mexico; Sharon from Aruba; Viviana from Chile; Andrés from Colombia; Gerardo from Paraguay; Aida and Stephen from China; Ana and Alejandro from Taiwan; Gita from India; Iris from Korea and Masako from Japan.

Thank you also to Vanesa Kandel and Yael Berman, who taught the Spanish classes during which I got the idea to start this project.

And Inés Marini, who gave me her support and the trust I needed to continue. Hanneke Vaanhold, for her contribution to the writing process and her faith in this unique project. And my editor, Carmen Güiraldes, who

117

helped me convey my thoughts and feelings in the right tone and in correct Spanish.

Last but not least, I want to thank my Dutch and Argentine families, my friends from Argentina and from abroad, my husband Alex and my children Nina, Sophie, Carmen and Tobias, who inspired me with their ideas and always believed my book would see daylight.

Bibliographical references

María Sáenz Quesada: *La Argentina, historia del país y de su gente*; Sudamericana, 2012 (2nd edition).

Jorge Lanata: ADN, Mapa genético de los defectos argentinos; Planeta, 2004.

Ted Stanger: Sacrés Français! Un américain nous regarde; folio documents 2003.

Leila Marcor: *Lamentablemente, estamos bien*; Debolsillo, 2009 (2nd edition).

Robert Hamwee: *Culture Smart! Argentina*; Kuperard, 2006.

Fiona Adams: *Culture Shock! Argentina;* Marshall Cavendish Editions, 2011 (4th edition).

Alejandro Grimson: *Mitomanías argentinas;* Siglo Veintiuno Editores, 2013.

Joanna Nowicki: La Cohabitation culturelle, Les Essentiels d'Hermès ; CNRS Éditions, 2009.

Ludovic Lamant: Les guides de l'état du monde Argentine; La Découverte, 2011.

Alejandra Laurencich: El taller, nociones sobre el oficio de escribir; Aguilar, 2014.

Carol Graham: *The pursuit of happiness: an economy of well-being*; Brookings Focus Books, Brookings Institution's Press, 2011.

Table of Content